FUCKING

GO FOR IT

INSIGHT
EDITIONS

SAN RAFAEL • LOS ANGELES • LONDON

Well, well, well, look who we have here.

Fed up with the daily grind, huh? Sick of work and stress and more work? Maybe you were doomscrolling through influencer Instagram, looking at all the spotless marble countertops and yoga stretches and free tropical vacations, and you thought, "Hey, I could use a little mindfulness." Or maybe you're just tired of everyone telling you what to do all the time and you want a little freedom to do things YOUR way.

Great. Let me tell you how to do this, and then you can fuck off and do it however you want.

This isn't just a regular coloring book. It's a *Coloring Adventure* book. Which means it's waaaayyyyy better than all those boring coloring books. Lucky you, huh? Here's what you do:

Step 1: Start on the first page.

Step 2: Read the page.

Step 3: Color the page.

Step 4: Choose your next action from the options.

Step 5: Go to the page you're directed to. (It might be page 2; it might be page 47. The world is full of endless possibilities!)

Step 6: Repeat steps 2 through 5 until you reach an end (where there are no more diverging actions to choose).

Step 7: Go back to the beginning (or to your last bad choice) and do it again.

Now, let's cut the shit. I can't make you do this right. I can't make you do anything. You could stop reading right now and go pick a random page to color. What can I say, your chaos is valid. But trust me, the best way to experience this book is to follow those steps. Otherwise, you might as well be coloring a kids' menu at a restaurant.

Have fun out there, and watch out for asshole birds.

Your alarm blares. 6 a.m. Another dawn, another drab day at your boring office job to look forward to. *Fuck.*

Before you leave the sweet, sweet sanctity of your warm bed, you tap your phone to check your work email. It's a bad habit, you know. Lo and behold, your Shitty Boss™ has asked you to come in early to help deal with an "urgent" task. *Goddamnit.*

What's your next move?

- ◼ Go back to sleep. Just five more minutes . . . **(Go to page 2.)**

- ◼ Jump out of bed! You're ready to KICK this task in the ASS, and anything else life throws at you today! **(Go to page 4.)**

- ◼ *Fuuuuuuu−* You're not happy about it, but you drag yourself out of bed and start getting ready. It's your boss—what other choice do you have? **(Go to page 5.)**

- ◼ Stare through your window at the rising sun as that familiar feeling of existential dread rises within you. The monotony of life—with no change in sight—mental breakdown in three . . . two . . . **(Go to page 6.)**

You sleep for five more minutes.
A small but blissful win. **(Return to page 1.)**

3

Your boss thanks you for coming in early, and the "urgent" task is repetitive but bearable. It's shaping up to be a decent morning . . . until your Annoying Coworker does The Thing. *Again.* Even though you've talked to them about this. And your teammate has talked to them about this. Even your boss has talked to them about this. *What do you do?*

■ Yell at them. **(Go to page 7.)**

■ Try to talk to them about it. **(Go to page 8.)**

■ Ignore them and focus on your work. You can only control what's in your control. **(Go to page 9.)**

As you brush your teeth, you shoot back an email confirming that you'll be into work soon. Your phone buzzes as you wipe the last of the toothpaste off your face. It's Shitty Boss™ again. They want you to get them a coffee on your way in.

Sigh.

You walk to the nearest coffee shop. It's a chain café, and they're usually pretty quick. Not today: the line goes out the door, there are only two baristas behind the counter, and the person behind you keeps hack-coughing on your shoulder. Today's gonna be a shit show, you can already tell.

Eventually you reach the front of the line and tell pimply-faced Liam that you'd like a black coffee and a frappuccino. You wait ten minutes. Then ten more. Liam drops a gallon of soy milk. Good thing you woke up early this morning. Five more and they call your name—but the order's wrong. Fifteen more minutes and another wrong order later, the manager, Lydia, comes out to apologize profusely . . . and blames everything on her lazy, sloppy employees.

Your first thought is . . .

- You know what? You're not going to be baited by the world today. You choose grace. You tip extra to the baristas and wait patiently for your coffee to be made correctly before heading into work. **(Go to page 4.)**

- Areeeeeeeee youuuuuuu fuuuuuuucking KIDDING WITH THIS SHIT!? LYDIA AND THE REST OF THE BULLSHIT BOSS BRIGADE CAN FUCK RIGHT OFF. You *get* your coffee, *stomp* to work, and *vow* to look into starting a union for all underserved employees. **(Go to page 17.)**

- This is . . . not worth it. You leave and go to the donut store next door instead. You've been wanting a change anyway. **(Go to page 20.)**

You're burned-out, you're tired, you really don't want to do this. If you have to go through ONE MORE DAY of this gray existence—something in you snaps. You can't. You WON'T.

Before your brain can catch up, your hands are moving to your phone. You:

■ Call in and fake sick. **(Go to page 19.)**

■ Email back that you'll show up at the regular time, but you're not coming in early. You need to work up to full rebel, OK? **(Go to page 17.)**

You scream at them so intensely that you literally explode with the fire of a thousand suns. You are dead, but your legacy at the company lives on: a bunch of people quit, and they can never get the scorch marks out of the carpet.

Bebster's dictionary gains a new entry under your name:

Verb.

To become so angry that you spontaneously combust.

(Return to page 4.)

You approach Annoying Coworker with a kind reminder and end up having a genuinely nice conversation! They're going through a tough time right now, and they really appreciate you checking in on them. People are flawed, and that's OK.

To thank you for being understanding, they offer to cover your workload for the rest of the day. Do you take their offer?

■ Uh, no. As much as you want to believe in them, they'd probably botch the job. **(Go to page 10.)**

■ Are you kidding? You're outta there! Time to get some fresh air! **(Go to page 11.)**

You work efficiently (if not happily) and finish earlier than expected. Shitty Boss™ is out meeting a client for the rest of the day, and you don't have any other pressing work to do. Maybe . . . you can leave early? With a covert glance around, you casually stroll down the hallway, out the door, and into . . .

Freedom! You take a deep breath, replacing the stale office air in your lungs with the sweet oxygen of the outdoors. Looking around, you see two tantalizing prospects: a local nature park, and a ferry that seems to cruise around a lake. The world is at your fingertips now.

Where will you go?

■ Lake Ferry! **(Go to page 12.)**

■ Park! **(Go to page 11.)**

You politely decline your coworker's offer and stay at work to finish out the day. Tragically, despite their best intentions, your coworker resumes their annoying behavior almost immediately. Goddamnit. You spend the rest of the day with a headache. **(Return to page 8.)**

It's a beautiful day to be at the park! The sky is a gorgeous blue and the sunlight is filtering through the leaves to create a magnificent canopy of green to shade you. Even better, you picked up a delicious sandwich and perfectly cooked fries on your way here. You find a clean bench with a view of a pond, and settle down to enjoy your amazing spread of food.

However. The world won't ever let you catch a fucking break.

As soon as you sit down, an enormous flock—nay, swarm—of birds descends upon you like a maelstrom. They're EVERYWHERE—in the trees, on the ground, in the air, in the pond. You're surrounded on all sides by the stupid cooing gits, and they won't leave you and your sandwich alone. How do you deal with them?

■ Deal with them? They're just birds; no need to overreact. **(Go to page 13.)**

■ Annoying PEOPLE are one thing, but you won't stand for these literal birdbrains. It's time to throw rocks. **(Go to page 14.)**

Weeeeell, this is awkward. See, you thought you boarded a ferry that toured the lake. Turns out, the ship you boarded was the *Lakeferry Ocean Cruiser*, a cruise liner that'll be traversing the high seas for the next few months. You try to tell the captain, but she shrugs and says there's nothing she can do. You can only watch as the familiar shoreline drifts farther and farther away . . .

You get used to life at sea. The food is good, the entertainment's great, and there's a poolside tiki bar on deck 3 with bottomless martinis. And what better excuse for not showing up to work than being held hostage on a ship for months?

There is one thing that makes you nervous: the captain is nice and charismatic, but you've noticed that she definitely spends more time giving dramatic retellings of her daring adventures at sea than actually steering the ship. You shrug it off at first; what do you know about ships? But then you overhear one sailor complaining to another, "At this rate, we really might crash!"

- Driving a car and driving a boat can't be that different, right? You're taking matters into your own hands! **(Go to page 15.)**

- Kick back and relax. Now that you're ON the cruise, there's not much you can do until you're back on land! **(Go to page 16.)**

If there's only one lesson you learn in your life, it's this: Never. Underestimate. Birds. They sense your apathy. Their tiny dinosaur brains interpret it as weakness.

They poop on you. It's gross. You don't have any tissues.

- ■ Sit on the bench and cry. **(Go to page 23.)**
- ■ Go somewhere to get tissues to clean the poop off. **(Go to page 24.)**

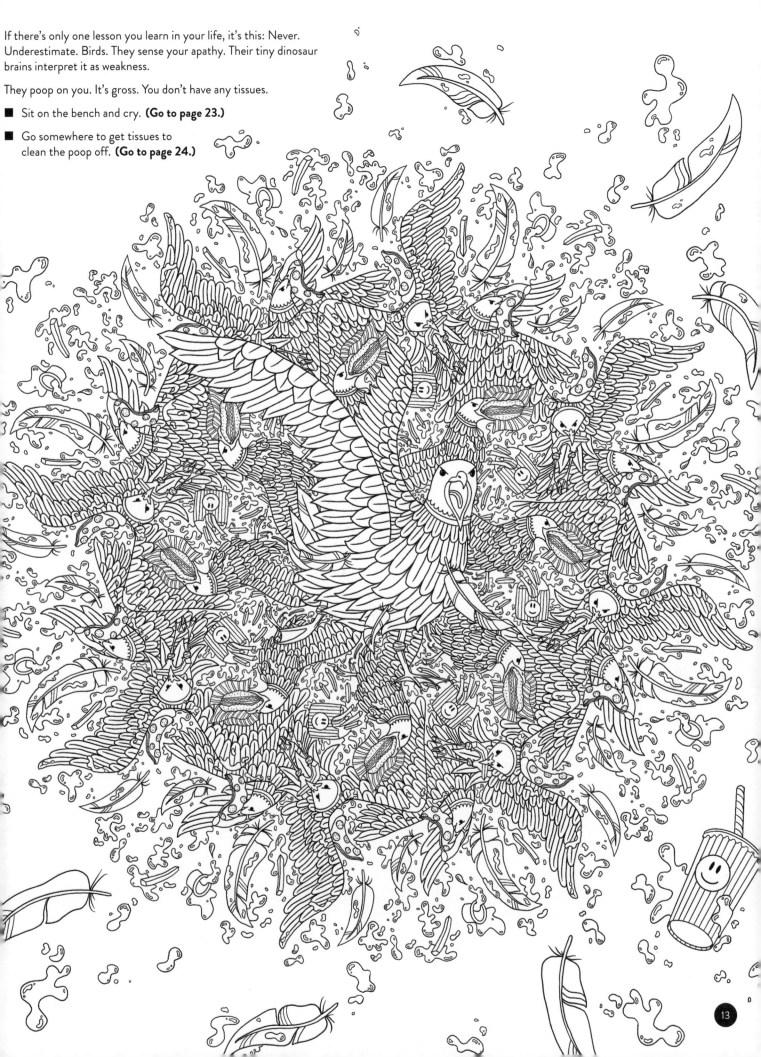

Quick as lightning, you snarf down your sandwich. You gather some pebbles and prepare to face these asshole wannabe dino descendants. You roar, and the leaves on the trees quiver. People around you look baffled and a little bit scared, BUT the birds fly away. For now. You've won this battle.

You're breathing heavily as the adrenaline fades. You realize you're sweating pretty heavily—from the heat of your sweater, or from your triumph, or maybe it was that sandwich meat? Whatever the reason, you smell pretty bad and you've gotta wash up fast.

■ Find a convenience store to clean up. **(Go to page 24.)**

■ Call your friend who lives close by and see if you can go to their house. **(Go to page 30.)**

Um, yeah, so, what the hell were you thinking? You know nothing about ships! The ocean cruiser crashes into a deserted island. Luckily, everyone survived, and you all drag yourselves to shore. There doesn't seem to be any way to get a rescue message out—you're surrounded by miles and miles of sparkling blue water.

The island would actually be a nice place to hang out if you weren't trapped! Its white sandy beach and lush forestation seem untouched by human hands. The captain seems to have some survival experience, and delegates tasks. Pretty soon, you have a working semblance of civilization going on with palm shelters, collections of fruit, and a firepit. Still, you'd rather be back where there's working plumbing and internet browsers.

As the days go by, you start to pull out your dead phone and tap it with your thumbs, remembering how sweet it was to summon a GIF of a dog riding a motorcycle or know immediately how tall the president of Bangladesh is. Then one day, you spot it: one of your fellow stranded passengers has a crank charger and a wireless router they've been hiding under their palm pillow! Your mind races: this could be the withdrawal cravings of an addict, or it could be exactly what you need . . .

- ■ Take the stuff and try to connect to the internet. **(Go to page 43.)**

- ■ Throw your electronics into the ocean once and for all. **(Go to page 44.)**

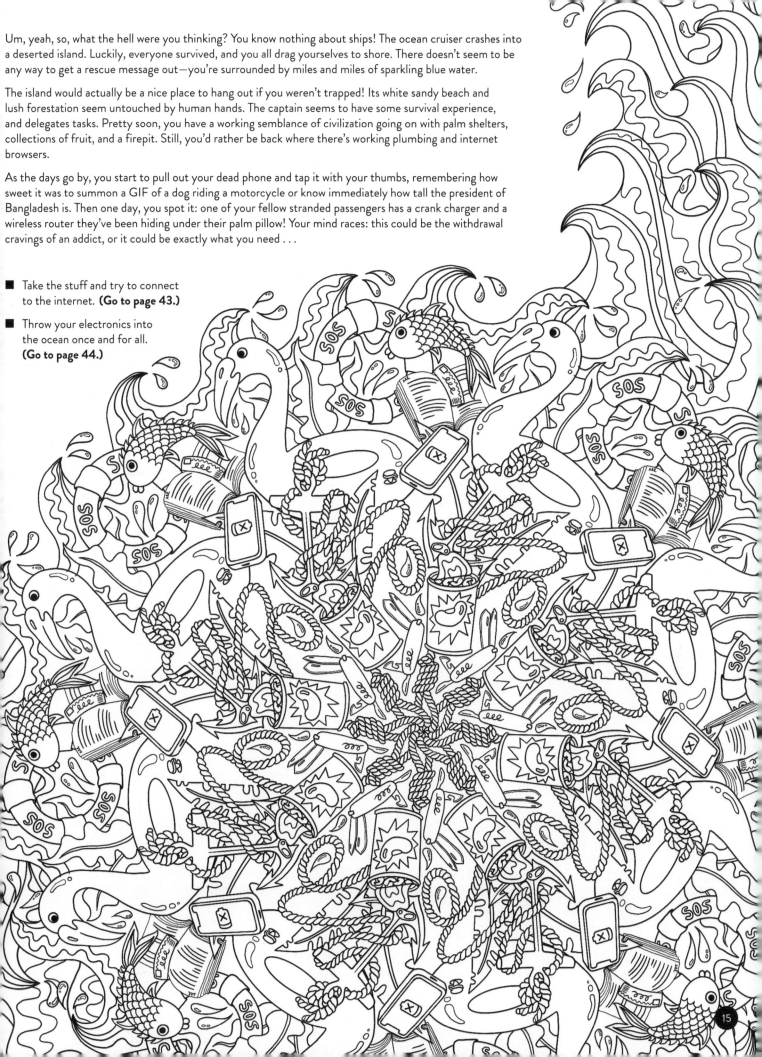

Turns out, choosing to just not worry is the solution sometimes. You enjoy a lovely three-month trip. When you come back, your boss fires you—fair enough, you were missing for three months and your entire office was freaking out—but you're feeling so relaxed and stress-free that you don't even mind. You sign up to work on the next ocean liner going out.

(Return to page 12.)

As soon as you get into work, Shitty Boss™ chews you out in front of the whole office for being late. They finish by demanding a list of deliverables from you that aren't even your responsibility. And they don't even say thank you for the coffee!

How do you retaliate?

- You don't. Anything you say to the face of authority will come back and bite you in the ass. Better to swallow your anger and just go sit at your desk. **(Go to page 47.)**

- Declare that as of immediately, you will be your own boss. Dare anyone to challenge you. **(Go to page 48.)**

17

You charge at your boss, and they charge at you. Unfortunately, neither of you knows how to throw a real punch. The slap-fight you have looks very silly, and eventually everyone gives up and goes home. **(Return to page 57.)**

You practice your best fake coughs and dial Shitty Boss's number. Miraculously, they believe you! You hang up and revel in your sudden freedom . . . and then you go back to sleep.

While in bed, you sleepily realize you need to pee. You pull yourself up to go to the bathroom, but right when you turn the knob on your bedroom door, you wake up. What a useless dream. You still need to pee, though, so you groggily get yourself up out of bed again—nope, that was a dream too.

Will you ever escape this surrealist hell!?

You continue to have repeating useless dreams, finally waking up after a nightmare where you call in fake sick to work. **(Return to page 6.)**

You eventually get to the office. You've no sooner set your stuff down on your desk when Shitty Boss™ strides over and threatens to fire you for being "uncooperative."

You take three deep, calming breaths, and:

- *Grovel.* It is extremely unfortunate, but you need money to live, and to make money you need this job. **(Go to page 21.)**
- *Quit.* If they think you're uncooperative, you'll SHOW them uncooperative. You never liked this job anyway; it's the perfect opportunity to take life by the horns and make a drastic change. **(Go to page 22.)**

You grovel. You grovel as you've never groveled before. You grovel like you're in the court of the Sun King. You grovel like you have the hopes and disappointments of all your dead ancestors weighing on your back. You set a new world record for world's best groveler. People will study your groveling for centuries to come. Your boss relents.

It's the lowest you've ever felt, but you still have a source of income. That's gotta mean something, right? Right??
(Return to page 20.)

You throw down your manila folders and binder clips, tell Shitty Boss™ to fuck all the way off, and storm out. It feels fantastic, and you spend the rest of the day listening to your power-anthem playlist. But the thing is . . . you still kind of need a steady inflow of cash. What are you going to do for your next gig: apply to jobs similar to the one you had, or try to totally change up your life and move abroad?

■ Stick with the familiar. It may not be the most exciting career move, but you know you'll be good at it. **(Go to page 34.)**

■ You want DRASTIC CHANGE! Time to chase your dreams and move. You don't know what awaits you, but this is the most alive you've felt in years. **(Go to page 35.)**

You sit on the bench and cry. It's kind of cathartic.
There's something beautiful about crying on a park bench
covered in bird shit. (Return to page 13.)

You walk to the convenience store on the nearest street corner to refresh yourself. You pick out some wet wipes and a bottle of water and are browsing magazines when suddenly—shit!— you see Shitty Boss™ walk in.

They haven't seen you yet. Do you duck into the candy aisle to try and avoid them, or say hi?

■ Avoid! Always avoid! **(Go to page 25.)**

■ Say hi. You don't think you've really done anything wrong! **(Go to page 26.)**

Ah, crap. Your boss sees you duck away and finds it suspicious. They start interrogating you on why you left early today and why you were avoiding them. You get roped into coming in early tomorrow to make up for stealing time. Back to the drawing board. **(Return to page 1.)**

You have no reason to run away from your boss! When they see you, they thank you for being a team player today; your work really helped them out when meeting the client! You already knew you did good work, but it's nice to be recognized and appreciated.

You chat with your boss for a while, and by the time they leave you realize it's later than you thought. You decide to pick something up for dinner too, but what?

- Ingredients to cook your favorite dinner! Might not be the healthiest, but you can indulge yourself now and then. **(Go to page 27.)**

- There's a new diet that all your buds in the group chat are trying: the kale-smoothie regimen, which seems to be just blended-up kale. So you get three bushels of kale. **(Go to page 28.)**

You have a lovely time cooking while jamming to your favorite playlist, and eat a filling, scrumptious dinner.

(Go to page 29.)

You try making the kale shake. Regrettably, it tastes like shit. You try to chug it all quickly, but you end up choking and have to be rushed to the emergency room for de-kale-ifying. Good luck with those medical bills. **(Return to page 26.)**

You sink into the soft luxury of your bed with a content sigh—you made great choices today, and can drift off to sleep feeling cozy, accomplished, and fulfilled. You'll be refreshed and relaxed when you wake up tomorrow, ready to live your best life through any fuckery.

The End... or return to page 1 and make different choices.

You call your friend, remembering a second too late that they're extremely dramatic. They answer the phone already in tears, and you manage to make out that they and their on-again-off-again partner are off again . . . for the fifth time in the last six months. Oh, no . . .

■ Let them rant and cry to you. **(Go to page 31.)**

■ Cut them short. You want to support your friend, but you don't have the patience for bullshit. **(Go to page 32.)**

Everyone should have a good shoulder to cry on when they need one. You spend the rest of your evening hearing the drama king out. You're exhausted, but at least you're a *good friend*. (Return to page 30.)

Listen, you're not going to enable your friend's toxic relationship. You kindly but firmly cut your friend off, reminding them that their relationship isn't healthy. They sniffle and agree, though you know there's still a 50/50 chance they'll actually break it off. Hey, at least you won't have to hear about it anymore.

You head home and shower to wash off the day, then have some leftover pasta for dinner. Before you know it, ten o'clock rolls around— but your other friend just texted you about this incredible new limited-series show that you HAVE to watch. You check your go-to streaming service: it's there. Six episodes, forty-five minutes each.

You *couuuuld* go to sleep . . . or you could stay up and binge-watch the whole show.

- ■ *Binge!* **(Go to page 33.)**
- ■ *Sleep.* **(Go to page 29.)**

BLITTISH BRAKE OFF

You know what? Sometimes bingeing IS self-care, and you're gonna watch *Blittish Brake Off* 'til the wee hours of the morning! You might regret it in six hours, but right now, this IS what you need. So, take that, haters. **(Return to page 32.)**

You get a job that matches your old job description. Things are almost eerily the same, but . . . something feels off. You're not exactly sure what . . .

Regardless, you fall back into the mundanity of everyday life. At least your boss is a little more reasonable and your coworkers are fine. **(Return to page 22.)**

Hell, yeah! You're moving abroad, like you've always dreamed of! And you have the perfect location picked out, the one you've always had in the back of your mind. You're so excited that the pains of relocating barely register!

You let your friends know, and your parents, and word gets around. Just as you're planning your travel logistics, your kooky aunt calls. She's got some VERY SPECIFIC and VERY PRESSING travel advice that all seems to come back to consulting one eccentric travel agent. It seems a bit dubious to you, to be honest. But hey, your aunt's lived longer than you and traveled a lot. Do you take her advice?

- ■ Sure! She may be wacky, but she has experience. (Go to page 36.)

- ■ Nah! You know what you're doing, and you're tired of doing what other people tell you to. Sorry, Auntie, but you'll plan your own trip. (Go to page 37.)

The travel agent is wearing a weird, woolly suit and smells like musty ginger, but generally seems to know what he's talking about. Which is good, because he talks a LOT: he drones on and on about the climate of your destination, and how to avoid mold in your new home, and the safety procedures of cargo ships. Finally, he gives you some pamphlets and some options: first, decide whether to travel by air or by sea.

You know which you'd prefer: you hate flying with a passion. But this is a new start, and maybe it's time to face your fears?

■ Travel by ship. You'll start doing new things once you get to the new place. **(Go to page 37.)**

■ Travel by plane! The old you was a scared little baby, but the new you isn't. **(Go to page 38.)**

You decide to travel by ship to your destination! The fresh, salty air wakes you up in the mornings and the gentle rocking of the waves lulls you to sleep every night. You meet some really interesting people from all walks of life. You've always known it: sometimes, the long route is the better one.

Aaaaand sometimes it's not. Halfway through the journey, your ship runs into a fucking TERRIFYING SEA STORM. The ship is rocking like an amusement park ride. You're hanging on to the railings for dear life. Can you do anything to keep the ship from capsizing??

- ■ Use the safety procedures you learned from the travel agent to take command and get the ship to safety! **(Go to page 44.)**

- ■ Safety procedure? What safety procedures?? You have no idea how to deal with a sea storm! What even IS a sea storm!? HELP HELP HELPHELPHELPHELP **(Go to page 15.)**

You buy that plane ticket! Unfortunately, facing your fear isn't the same thing as overcoming your fear: the flight scares the living shit out of you. Somehow, though, you manage to make it to your destination without puking! You're feeling super confident as you take your first steps in your new homeland.

Your confidence must show, because almost immediately you're approached by a handsome man who looks troubled. He explains to you that he's a foreign prince stranded at this airport and begs you for some cash to get in touch with his royal guard. It's not an extraordinary amount. Do you lend him some?

■ Eh, what the heck. Sure, you can spare him a twenty. **(Go to page 41.)**

■ Uh, you were born at night, but it wasn't LAST night. Get this con artist away from you. **(Go to page 42.)**

COZYFLIX
AND CHILL

Nothing like a familiar taste to make you feel welcome in a new place! Munching on this brings back memories of watching your favorite bad sitcom. You pull up an episode and watch it on your laptop. It's nice to hold on to good things from your past as you make your way into a promising future! **(Return to page 42.)**

You throw on an old hoodie and head out to a local market. There are so many new types of foods you can't wait to try, but you settle on picking just one thing you've definitely never had before. It smells . . . er, interesting.

As you get home and get your keys out to unlock your front door, someone calls out to you. You turn; it's your neighbor, and they're waving excitedly at you. They introduce themselves as also from your old hometown. You look down and realize your hoodie says the name of your high school. Oof. Now you're in unending conversation with this well-meaning neighbor who stands too close and doesn't seem very aware of the time.

- Be curt, cut them off, and lock your front door behind you. You've gotta set boundaries with these types of people. **(Go to page 45.)**

- Feign interest, but ward them off with your smelly food. **(Go to page 46.)**

In a strange turn of events, the stranded man turned out to actually be a real prince! After he makes it safely back to his home, he reaches out to thank you. He grants you eternal favors, and you live out the rest of your life amid high society. You constantly have to deal with lavish aristocratic parties. Condolences.

(Return to page 38.)

You brush past the con artist and head to your new place. A good start to your new life does NOT include getting scammed out of hard-earned cash. You want to spend it on furniture for your new place instead.

You have a grueling but productive moving day. Once everything is set up, you collapse on your new couch. Your stuff looks awesome, but you can't appreciate it because your stomach is threatening to eat itself. After all that physical labor, you're starving. What's your first meal in your new home going to be?

■ Go for something familiar! Comfort food never fails.
  (Return to page 39.)

■ Try some local cuisine. After all, this is what you came here for!
  (Return to page 40.)

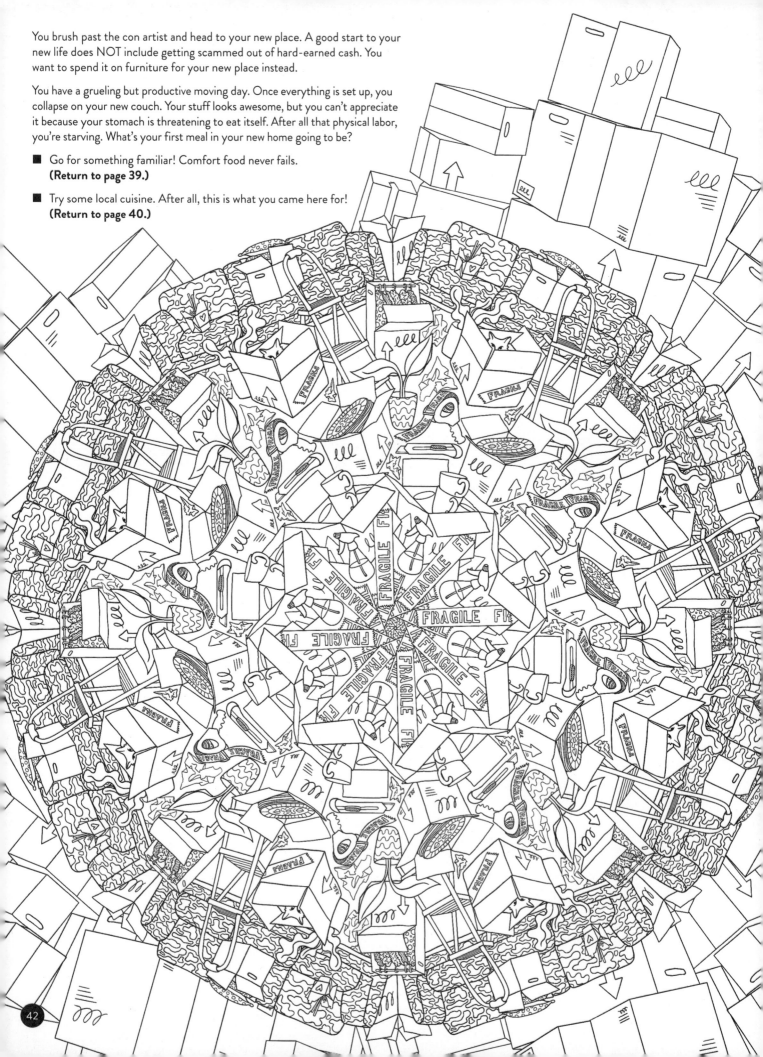

You work through the night, forcing yourself to recall any information that you absorbed from your friend in IT. Finally, you get the router powered and connected—and by some stroke of divine luck, the WiFi signals one bar! But when you click to connect, a window pops up: "Please enter the password."

You try "1234." You try "12345." You try "Password." *Nothing works.*

RRRRRAAAAAAAAAAAAAAAAGHHHHHHHHHHHHHHHHKKKKKKK

In your rage, you smash the router into pieces. Your screams die in the wind. By daybreak, you're all raged out. You walk back to the camp, defeated. You spend the rest of your life in relative comfort and peace, though your fingers twitch in the dead of night, longing for a vestigial phone they will never tap the buttons of again.

(Return to page 15.)

What a huge success! You've changed your life entirely and navigated the stress of change and novelty really well in your new home. Maybe there were ups, downs, and surprises, but every day feels like a new adventure, and it's all possible because you took those first steps.

The End . . . or return to page 1 and make different choices.

Your neighbor is bewildered as you abruptly open your door and walk inside. Just before the door slams, you see their expression change to disgruntled. Get ready to live with some pissed-off neighbors for your remaining time here. **(Return to page 40.)**

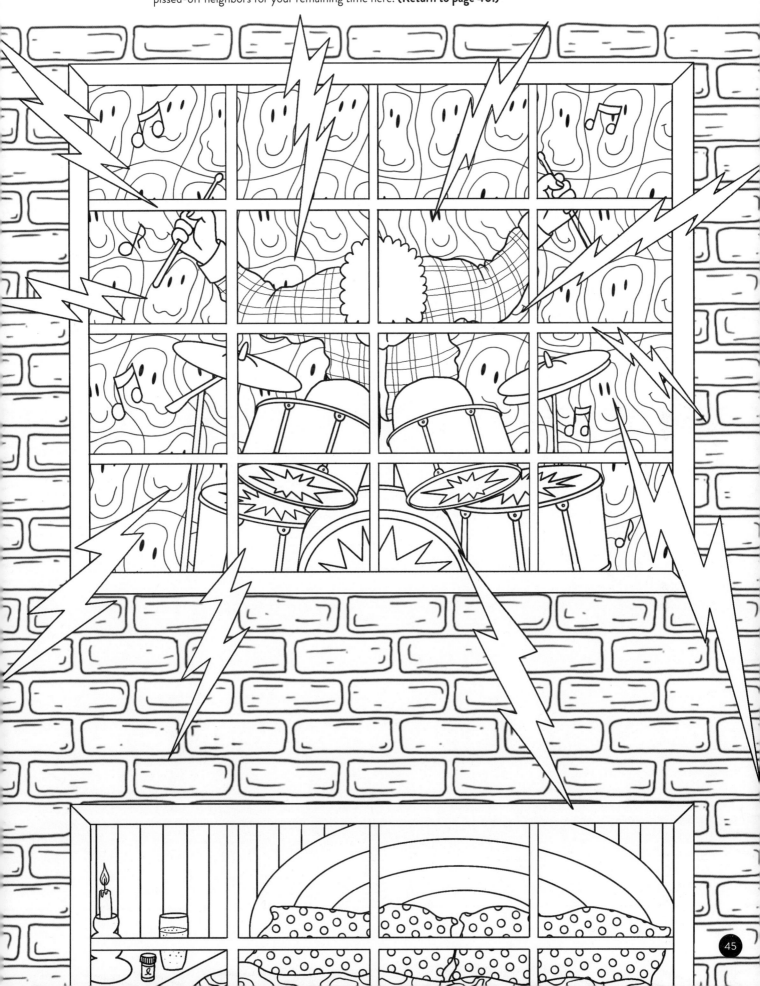

Ha-HA! You nod politely but take out your container of very strong-smelling food and start eating it while your neighbor talks. You do your best to waft it their way. Your neighbor makes a face and excuses themselves.

Genius! You're freaking brilliant! Also, the food tastes great!
(Go to page 44.)

You sit down at your gray desk. Gray computer, gray pens, gray cubicle walls. The world just looks so dull and drab today. The fire you felt this morning feels distant in the light of the oppressive tedium of your daily life and the overwhelming, pervasive issues of the system.

■ Welp, nothing to it. Start the list of tasks your boss assigned you. **(Return to page 49.)**

■ You can't take it anymore; quit your job! You can't let mundanity dictate the rest of your life. **(Return to page 22.)**

■ You'll do what you can with the means you have. Secretly start to research how to unionize. **(Go to page 50.)**

Your boss is clearly furious, but your coworkers and teammates are awestruck by your bravery and fortitude. They band around you and commiserate, and you learn about a whole lot of shit the company's been doing that you had no idea about.

The desire to revolt grows, and your allies are looking to you for what to do next.

- This is a lot of information to take in all of a sudden; you need to take a breather. **(Go to page 11.)**

- Let's make this a covert operation. You direct everyone to focus their attention on helping minimum wage employees. **(Go to page 50.)**

- The leaders have been taking advantage of you all for TOO FUCKING LONG! This office will be the battleground of a REVOLUTIONARY ARMY! Build a barricade! **(Go to page 51.)**

You still have your job, and that's the most important thing. You sit down and start your work. An hour passes. Then two. The rest of the day. And the week. The month, the year, the century.

The year 2070 rolls around. You're at your desk, working away. Your limbs have been replaced by mechanical parts. Your boss is an automated soda dispenser. On your break, you wheel down to the neo-coffeeshop and order an Americano with two pumps of oil. They get your order wrong.

Life goes on. You sigh and wonder what would have happened if you'd stood up to your boss all those years ago. **(Return to page 47.)**

The office begins to resume the appearance of everyday mundanity, but though you look like you're typing away at your reports, you're rapidly researching unions on the down-low. You reach out to a lawyer who has a great reputation and is willing to help. Just as you've hit Send on a very productive and union-based email, the CEO of your company materializes out of NOWHERE and starts toward your cubicle with a mean look in their eye. Your annoying coworker must have ratted you out—you brace for impact.

However, as your CEO takes one last menacing step toward you, they trip and fall on their face. Everyone in the office freezes. What do you do?

- Put your face on the floor as well, and grovel for your job. **(Return to page 49.)**

- Offer your CEO a hand up. **(Go to page 52.)**

- Chance advantage! There's no use hiding anymore: take this opportunity of your enemy's weakness to rally allies for the underserved! **(Go to page 51.)**

Together, you and your team break down cubicle walls and office chairs and pack them into a barricade that none of your managers can bypass. The customer service team builds a safeguarded tunnel to a back stairwell that connects directly to a cafeteria downstairs so you have plenty of food, and the IT team changes the passwords for all the internet routers so you can get messages in and out to your families. You all agree on a strict rule: no one crosses the barricade until the bosses give you better working conditions.

After weeks of being at a standstill, your manager asks to meet you in a neutral zone. They offer you amnesty—but just you, not your comrades. Do you take the deal?

- ■ This has gone further than you ever planned, and it scares you. You have to take the out. **(Go to page 53.)**

- ■ Betray all your comrades?! FUCK NO. **(Go to page 54.)**

Your CEO breaks down crying. The sentiment of your gesture—no one has shown them that kindness in years. They start telling you all about the choices that got them here; how their kids barely know them, how they quit smoking cigarettes two years ago and haven't felt complete since. After four hours, they weepily agree to moderately better conditions for their employees.

Job well done! Will you give yourself a breather, or stay and navigate the new world you've negotiated for?

- Stay—you've got to see this through. **(Go to page 55.)**

- Four hours of being your CEO's therapist was a LOT. Take a breather. **(Go to page 11.)**

IT WAS A STING!

(Return to page 51.)

53

You refuse the deal. Now, the execs are calling in reinforcements. Who knew your CEO was connected to the army and crazy scientists? Your fellow employees look to you for orders.

■ Suit up for battle; you can't ask your followers to do something you won't. **(Go to page 56.)**

■ Decode the enemy's secret message and use their power against them. **(Go to page 57.)**

You choose to stay and navigate a world with better benefits. You've got a slightly increased rate of pay—not quite enough to cover inflation, of course, but close—a better copay for doctor's appointments ($100 instead of $110), and you even get one whole flex holiday! Your CEO is impressed, and leans on you as they make changes for the future.

But even though the change is happening, it's slow. You see holes in the system that you know you could fix, but the CEO seems resistant to change. Eventually, though, they offer you a promotion. A really good one. You'd be in charge of a lot of people, you'd have a big, cushy office setup, and your salary would be out the wazoo. The only thing is, you know that if you take it, you'd be expected to not push the envelope.

■ Take the promotion. You've earned it, and the things you've done so far should be enough. **(Go to page 58.)**

■ You can't sell out your beliefs! Refuse the promotion. **(Go to page 59.)**

You bravely march out on the front lines, but pretty quickly you're stomped on by a kaiju-sized sheep. You died as a hero for your cause, but you probably would've been of more use if you'd stayed alive. Sometimes it's better not to unnecessarily martyr yourself. **(Return to page 54.)**

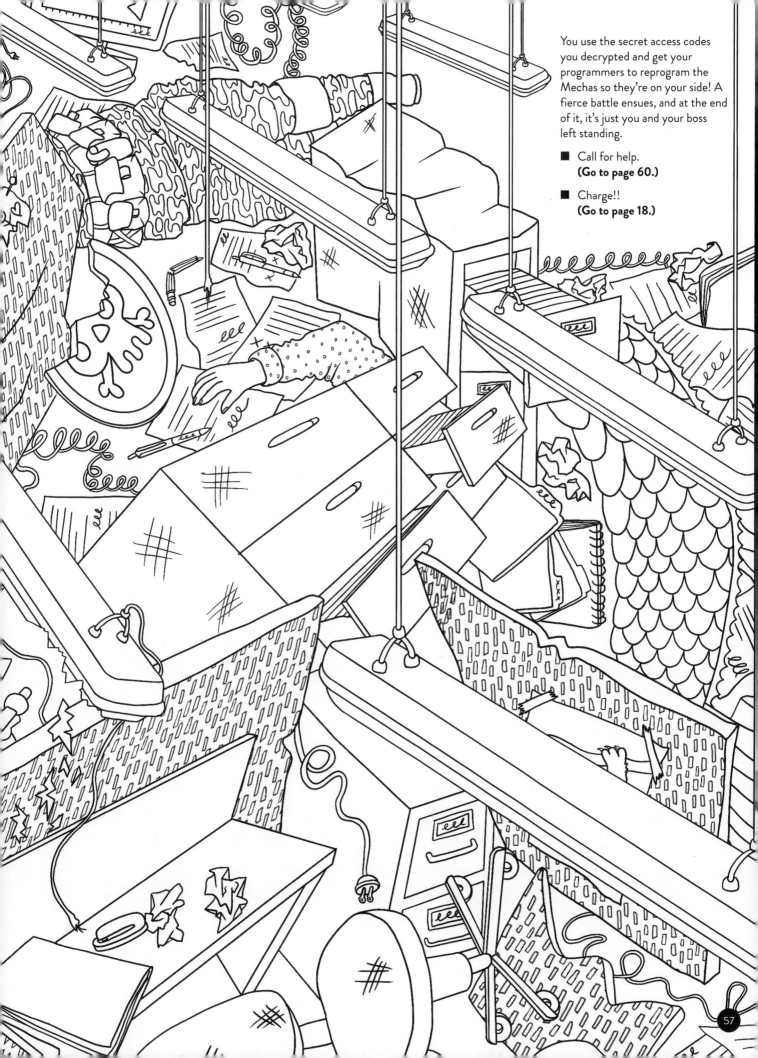

You use the secret access codes you decrypted and get your programmers to reprogram the Mechas so they're on your side! A fierce battle ensues, and at the end of it, it's just you and your boss left standing.

■ Call for help.
(Go to page 60.)

■ Charge!!
(Go to page 18.)

You've made it! Or have you? As you sink into your ergonomic office chair, it hits you: while fighting against the authorities, you've become what you hated. Now YOU are the authoritarian telling other people what to do, when really, you have no idea what you're doing.

You live the rest of your life in wealth, but the philosophical crisis haunts you.

The End. . . . or return to page 1, make different choices, and Continue Your Adventure!

You refuse the promotion and recommit to making positive change in the system. The next week, your CEO has a sudden heart attack and dies! You take on the leadership spot in their stead.

As CEO, you find that it's a lot harder to run a company than it seems from the bottom, but you do your best to keep it healthy and nontoxic. Good job, you.

The End. . . . or return to page 1, make different choices, and Continue Your Adventure!

You're on your last legs. Your shaking fingers have just enough strength in them to tap a desperate call for help into your phone before the device falls from your hands. The sun is directly above the wrecked remains of your office building.

You take a steadying breath. In one pocket you have your employee handbook, in the other, your right-to-unionize documents. Shitty Boss™ is breathing steam. It's just you and them left. It's always been you and them. It's time to finish this.

But Shitty Boss™ is faster than you. This whole time, they've been protecting themselves by letting others take the fall for them. They whip out a giant megaphone and your heart sinks. You already know what's going to happen.

"YOU. ARE. FIRE—"

A hiss, and their voice is muffled! You look around wildly, and it's beautiful: all around you, a wall of generic chain store coffee employees has come to your rescue. They've blocked the megaphone with extra whipped cream. They're weighing Shitty Boss™ down with caramel-and-chocolate croissants. Pimply Liam gives you a thumbs-up.

You, and all the other low-salary employees, have won. You've triumphed over an unjust system. You are victorious. All that's left is to go home and take a well-earned nap.

The End.

. . . or return to page 1, make different choices, and continue your adventure!

INSIGHT
EDITIONS

PO Box 3088
San Rafael, CA 94912
www.insighteditions.com

f Find us on Facebook: www.facebook.com/InsightEditions
🐦 Follow us on Twitter: @insighteditions
📷 Follow us on Instagram: @insighteditions

ISBN: 979-8-88663-320-7

Publisher: Raoul Goff
VP, Co-Publisher: Vanessa Lopez
VP, Creative: Chrissy Kwasnik
VP, Manufacturing: Alix Nicholaeff
VP, Group Managing Editor: Vicki Jaeger
Publishing Director: Mike Degler
Art Director: Catherine San Juan
Executive Editor: Jennifer Sims
Editorial Assistant: Alex Figueiredo
Managing Editor: Maria Spano
Senior Production Editor: Michael Hylton
Production Associate: Tiffani Patterson
Senior Production Manager, Subsidiary Rights: Lina s Palma-Temena

Written by Erin Kwong • Illustrations by Rachel Winter

ROOTS of PEACE   🌲 REPLANTED PAPER

Insight Editions, in association with Roots of Peace, will plant two trees for each tree
used in the manufacturing of this book. Roots of Peace is an internationally renowned humanitarian
organization dedicated to eradicating land mines worldwide and converting war-torn lands into productive
farms and wildlife habitats. Roots of Peace will plant two million fruit and nut trees in Afghanistan and
provide farmers there with the skills and support necessary for sustainable land use.

Manufactured in China by Insight Editions

10 9 8 7 6 5 4 3 2 1